D0371679

FORAGER'S COCKTAILS

BOTANICAL MIXOLOGY WITH FRESH, NATURAL INGREDIENTS

AMY ZAVATTO

STERLING EPICURE
New York

For the much-missed Virginia Zavatto, who allowed her beautiful honeysuckle to be decimated so that, drop by drop, her youngest could attempt (unsuccessfully) to fill a Dixie cup with that wildflower's delicious liquid. You never discouraged me from the impossible—and so I thought anything was possible. Even honeysuckle cocktails.

STERLING EPICURE
New York

An Imprint of Sterling Publishing
1166 Avenue of the Americas
New York, NY 10036

STERLING EPICURE is a trademark of Sterling Publishing Co., Inc.
The distinctive Sterling logo is a registered trademark of Sterling Publishing Co., Inc.

First published in 2015 by Sterling Publishing, by arrangement with HarperCollins*Publishers*

Text copyright © 2015 Amy Zavatto

Images © Shutterstock pages i, 13, 20, 25, 41, 53, 57, 67, 69, 77, 85, 89, 91, 109, 111, 119, and 125. Alamy © page 7.
iStockphoto © page 15. Cover: canvas texture and foliage © Shutterstock.

All rights reserved. No part of this publication may be reproduced, stored in a retrieval system,
or transmitted in any form or by any means (including electronic, mechanical, photocopying,
recording, or otherwise) without prior written permission from the publisher.

ISBN 978-1-4549-1747-2

Concept creator and stylist: Caitlin Doyle
Cover and interior photographer: Claire Lloyd Davies
Cover and interior designer: Jacqui Caulton
Illustrations on pages 1, 31, 75, and 107 by Joe Bright

Distributed in Canada by Sterling Publishing
c/o Canadian Manda Group, 664 Annette Street
Toronto, Ontario, M6S 2C8, Canada

For information about custom editions, special sales, and premium and corporate purchases,
please contact Sterling Special Sales at 800-805-5489 or specialsales@sterlingpublishing.com.

Manufactured in China

2 4 6 8 10 9 7 5 3 1

www.sterlingpublishing.com

DISCLAIMER:
Please forage responsibly. Foraging rules and restrictions vary by country, and it is essential that
readers be aware of their own regional and national laws. Be safe and sensible in both foraging and
alcohol consumption. The publisher does not accept responsibility for misuse of any ingredients
or recipes given in this book, which are intended for use in moderation.

Some of the recipes in this book contain raw eggs. Consuming raw or undercooked eggs
may increase your risk of food-borne illness. The young, elderly, pregnant women, and
anyone who may be immunocompromised should not consume them.

CONTENTS

———◆◆◆———

FOREWORD

Have you ever had the pleasure of picking a ripe new strawberry directly from the patch, ruby red and so perfumed that your brain goes into overdrive with giddy anticipation before you even put it in your mouth? That sense of freshness once bitten, as juice dribbles down my chin, is one of the purest joys I can imagine!

Over the last 40 years, the gastronomic arc in America has evolved from a keen and then purposeful awareness of sustainably grown food to an equally passionate interest in wine, craft beer, and finally, and more recently, cocktails.

In many ways, the cocktail hobbyist has taken full hold of the zealous American history of cocktails, which has been researched and celebrated widely over the last decade, and applied the parameters of fresh and sustainable food to mixing delicious drinks. If chefs can have rooftop gardens from which to select the most pristine vegetables and herbs, why can't we treat our home-grown and locally sourced ingredients in much the same way as we fashion a refreshing libation?

My support of the Slow Food Movement in the United States coincided, in the early years of this young century, with the rise of the rejuvenated cocktail culture that has now stretched to communities and countries far and wide. In those days, not so long ago, even the concept of fresh juice behind the bar was not nearly as prevalent as it is today. The championing of quality ingredients—distilled spirits and modifiers, tinctures from herbs and teas, varieties of antique and contemporary bitters, and, yes, near ubiquity of fresh juice—mixed with the emergence of the professional bartender has created the perfect environment for cocktail enthusiasts to take advantage of the best of all aspects of our now-celebrated gastronomic interests.

This pleasure of creativity—whether at home or in our favorite cocktail bar—is not necessarily about convenience, but about discovery. The desire to create "wild cocktails" is a move away from industrial ingredients and a unique and, frankly, privileged pleasure to connect with the very components that comprise our daily food and drink.

There is a uniquely human connection to our sense of reason and desire. Whether you fancy home-grown or foraged herbs, or fruits and herbs from your local farmers' market, the opportunity to create the exciting, delicious, and unique cocktails crafted in these pages is sure to offer delight, occasional surprise, and, most of all, refreshment.

Cheers!

Allen Katz
Founder of the New York Distilling Company

INTRODUCTION

INTO THE WILD

Living in any urban area, you wouldn't think you have a lot of opportunity for foraging—and, well, sometimes foraging in a large metropolis simply means finding the one open grocery that has milk for your coffee in the morning.

But as long as there's sun and rain, dirt and seed, and root, it really is hard to keep a good plant down. I've lived in New York City since 1986, when I moved here to go to college, having sprung from a small island town where my mom sometimes sent me to the farm stand around the corner for supper's side dish. To say I had culture shock when I moved to New York City is an understatement. Here, it wasn't the woods that were the wilds but the Lower East Side and, at that point in history, unexplored areas of the outer boroughs—where foraging had more to do with cheap drinks, cute boys, and good bands.

About 12 years ago, I bit the bullet and bought a home with my husband in a hilly little neighborhood of Staten Island near that borough's public ferry. It is an area that's at once urban but also offers some more space for those of us tired of being stacked up in apartment-building boxes. For the first time in twenty-five years, I had a backyard—and a very overgrown one at that, since my home had been abandoned for many years before we decided to root in and give it some spit and polish. Back then, everything looked like a weed to me. And, to be fair, a lot of it probably technically was. The first wild plant that stood out among the rest, as much for its stubborn, rooted countenance as its incredible smell when I finally wrenched it loose from the earth, was sassafras saplings. It smelled like ... bubble gum! And Fruit Loops cereal. And a little like root beer soda. This dirty, gnarled, funny-looking root of this irksome, incredibly prolific weed turned out to be pretty awesome for cocktails. (You can use the leaves for the secret ingredient in gumbo, too—but that's a recipe for another time.)

I looked at the world a little differently after that. Spiky leaves springing off dandelions, that suburban arch-nemesis, looked like salad or perhaps something to pop off and pickle. When I went out to eastern Long Island in the summer months, where I grew up, I searched the sandy brush for beach plums, which I knew would make a beautiful garnish, liqueur, or syrup. Wild onions springing from the ground? Martini accompaniments, of course.

Putting fresh ingredients in your cocktails isn't just a fun weekend experiment; it also makes your drinks better. From the days of the Carthusian monks, reaping a multitude of herbs from their monastic grounds and putting them into tinctures and liqueurs (the original wild cocktail concocteurs!) for countenance-curing endeavors, the idea of preserving harvestables with spirits is an old trick that has become new again. It's thanks to both the thirty-year-old Slow Food Movement and the economic downturns of the early twenty-first century for sprouting the now-avid DIY movement of entrepreneurial tinkerers. But regardless of how we've started to re-adapt a thriftier, let's-get-real point of view, it's pretty exciting to see so many of us kicking pre-fab, mystery-made, store-bought products to the curb in favor of honest-to-goodness identifiable ingredients. No one's going to proclaim cocktails a health drink any time soon, but using real, fresh, good ingredients in them is a whole lot better (and more delicious) than high-fructose whatever. Good riddance to that.

I am not a professional forager. There are people who do really great work in that realm—many right here in my own city. "Wildman" Steve Brill, Marie Viljeon, Ava Chin are among my favorites (each of whom has a terrific book or two, and I highly recommend you pick them up). I am, if anything, a cocktail tinkerer and abundantly enthusiastic home cook—and this is how I implore you to approach this topic, too. Use this book for inspiration. Be curious. There is nothing more rewarding than using your imagination and integrating a forlorn piece of flora into a glorious gastronomic bit of sipping pleasure. Be careful, too: the plants I list here are all pretty safe bets; turn to the pros like those listed above or other foraging tomes for your area before ingesting something with which you are unfamiliar. Plants, berries, and mushrooms can be a boon to your cocktail shaker, but they can also be poisonous if you mistakenly opt for an unfriendly look-alike to the thing you really wanted. Curiosity and caution are your two best friends.

Don't ignore the more domesticated side of fresh ingredients, either: your pots of herbs, your prized summer tomato garden, a funny tuft of leafy greens at your local farmers' market that you have never seen or used before. Challenge yourself. What's the worst thing that can happen—you make a bad drink? You'll make a better one next time. The great thing about booze? Unlike the fresh ingredients I encourage you to incorporate here, its shelf life is fairly indefinite.

Be brave, be curious, get your hands dirty, and by all means do me the honor of having fun with this book. May you never look at weeds the same way again!

SPRING

<hr/>

I happen to be a little impartial about spring for selfish reasons—my birthday falls on the first day of it. That's sort of the point of the season, right? Things coming to life; each tree bud and crocus shoot an awakening, as if the world were opening its eyes, giving a big yawn and stretch, and saying, "Hey, what are we going to do today?" The possibilities are open and endless. That's what spring feels like in the botanical world: one big possibility. Maybe dandelions don't have to be treated as weeds. Maybe those wild onion shoots don't need to be mowed over but instead pulled from the ground and given a whole new purpose. And those early, curling fern bits? Oh, there's a lot you can do with those. True foragers see the spring season through a wide-angle lens that for the rest of us is a mere pinhole. But the great thing about spring? We get the chance to start all over again and discover things we never knew existed. I'm still learning; I hope this chapter encourages you to shake up a little curiosity for what's around you, too.

DANDELION PICKLE BACK

No other plant better represents the battle between the human desire for a perfect landscape and complete weedy chaos than the dandelion. Their craggy leaves and long-stemmed golden flowers shoot from the ground in complete defiance of suburban aesthetics, like a plant revolution that will never say die. But the thing about dandelions? They're delicious! Instead of seeing them as the ultimate insolent maverick, see them as a generous source of side dishes and, for our purposes, cocktail ingredients. You can use the lovely chive flower for this recipe, too. ☞

1½ ounces (45ml) bourbon
1 pickled dandelion or chive flower*

Pour the whiskey into a shot glass. Top with a pickled flower. Shoot the contents.

*Pickled Dandelions or Chive Flowers
1 cup (roughly 100g) dandelion or chive flowers,
gently rinsed and allowed to dry thoroughly
1 quart (approx. 1 liter) white wine vinegar

Add the clean, dry flowers to a quart-sized (1-liter) mason jar. Fill with vinegar. Place in a cool, dark place for 5 to 7 days.

———◆◆———

WILD ONION GIMLET

When I was a kid playing in the backyard, I used to like to grab the skinny, green, scallionlike stalks of wild spring onions from the ground and pry them free. Then I cut off the tops, plopped the the onion bulbs into my doll's supermarket cart, and let them have some real, live produce, not the plastic stuff they came with. That's still how I feel about these onions—why buy some unknown supermarket source of cocktail garnish when I've got fresh, perfectly sized, beautiful, gimlet-ready onions right in my own backyard? Go dig up some onions, and make this easy-peasy cocktail accoutrement. ☞

Wild onions

2½ ounces (75ml) London dry gin
½ ounce (15ml) dry vermouth
1 pickled wild spring onion*

Fill a mixing glass half-full with ice cubes. Pour in the gin and vermouth. Stir for 30 to 45 seconds. Strain into a coupe or cocktail glass, and garnish with a pickled wild spring onion.

*Pickled Wild Spring Onions
6–12 wild onions, washed, leaving just a little green tail
1½ cups (355ml) white wine vinegar
½ cup (120ml) water
1 tablespoon (15g) sugar
1 teaspoon (5g) kosher salt
1 sprig of dill
1 teaspoon (5g) juniper berries
1 teaspoon (5g) black peppercorns

Add the onions (I like to leave a little tail on them), vinegar, water, sugar, and salt to a pot and simmer for about 2 minutes. Allow to cool. Drop the dill, juniper berries, and peppercorns in a 16-ounce (475ml) mason jar and pour in the vinegar solution and onions. Store in the sealed jar in the refrigerator for up to 6 months.

LOCUST POCUS

Black locust trees in the spring are some of the most beautiful examples of the season—and the most prolific. They're everywhere in North America and Europe, even if you haven't noticed them before. This normally humble, craggy-bark tree busts out with tumbling bouquets of blossoms, white-petaled and pinkish at the bottom. The best part: they are edible and both mild and gently sweet. It's the way things should taste in spring. Like any flower, edible locust blossoms are fleeting, which is why I like embellishing something sparkling with them. There's an urgency to sparkling wine—the bubbles rising quickly as if they can't fly to the top fast enough. It's the ultimate embrace-the-moment embodiment. As to the homemade grenadine: you can use this for lots of things, both alcoholic and not (and in cooking, too). It's thoroughly worth whipping up a batch. And feel free to nosh on the blossoms after you sip on this. ☞

Black locust blossoms

½ ounce (15ml) homemade grenadine*
½ ounce (15ml) freshly squeezed lemon juice
4 ounces (120ml) sparkling wine (brut-level dryness recommended)
1 black locust blossom, for garnish

Pour the grenadine and lemon juice into a champagne flute. Top with sparkling wine and garnish with a locust blossom.

*Grenadine
¾ cup (150g) sugar
1 cup (235ml) unsweetened pomegranate juice

In a saucepan, combine the sugar and juice over medium heat, stirring until the sugar starts to dissolve. Simmer, stirring, for 5 to 7 minutes. Allow to cool. Store in an airtight jar in the refrigerator for up to a month.

NOTE: Feel free to play around with your grenadine, adding other herbs or fruit to the mix. In the summer, I like throwing in ¼ cup (20g) of chopped rose hips.

VIOLET LADY

This riff on the classic Pink Lady cocktail is easy enough to make pink instead if you prefer—just swap in rose-petal syrup. But I like the way the vibrant purple adds a twist to this tipple. Note that to make the egg whites really frothy, you should first do something called dry shaking. That is, shake the ingredients vigorously *without* the ice, then add the ice and shake again to chill it down and give the cocktail the requisite amount of dilution. ☞

Wild violets

1 egg white
¾ ounce (22ml) London dry gin
¾ ounce (22ml) freshly squeezed lemon juice
¾ ounce (22ml) apple brandy
¾ ounce (22ml) violet syrup*
1 violet flower or candied violets (and optional violet leaf), for garnish

Drop the egg white into a cocktail shaker without ice. Pour in the gin, lemon juice, apple brandy, and syrup. Shake for 25 to 30 seconds or until frothy. Add ice, and shake again for about 20 seconds. Strain slowly into a cocktail or coupe glass. Garnish with a fresh violet flower or candied violets.

*Violet Syrup
1½ cups (355ml) water
¾ cup (150g) sugar
1 cup (80g) violet flowers

In a saucepot, simmer the sugar and water over medium heat, stirring, until the sugar starts to dissolve. Add the flower petals, and simmer 5 to 7 minutes. Allow to cool. Transfer to a sealed container, and refrigerate for up to a month.

WELCOME WAGON

The pineapple likely became a symbol of hospitality from the days when this coniferous fruit was brought on merchant vessels near and far. But the pineapple weed actually has more in common with its close cousin chamomile (for which it is sometimes mistaken, sans the petals) than it does with the spiny, tropical fruit in its name. It does, however, smell an awful lot like pineapple. As to the weed part of its title—well, one man's weed is another's delicious cocktail ingredient. ☛

Pineapple weed

5 mint leaves
¾ ounce (22ml) pineapple weed syrup*
2 ounces (60ml) vodka
Club soda
1 sprig of pineapple weed or mint, for garnish

Drop the mint leaves in the bottom of a cocktail shaker, drizzle in a little of the pineapple weed syrup, and gently muddle. Fill the cocktail shaker half-full with ice, and pour in the vodka and the rest of the syrup. Shake for 25 to 30 seconds. Strain slowly into an ice-filled Collins glass or frosted tin cup. Top with club soda, and garnish with a sprig of pineapple weed or mint.

*Pineapple Weed Syrup
¾ cup (150g) sugar
1 cup (235ml) water
1 cup (80g) fresh pineapple weed, tops only

In a saucepot, gently simmer the sugar and water over medium heat, stirring, until the sugar starts to dissolve. Add the pineapple weed, and simmer, stirring, for 7 to 10 minutes. Allow to cool. Transfer to a sealed container, and refrigerate for up to a month.

NOTE: Also known as wild chamomile, pineapple weed can be difficult to find outside of North America and Northeast Asia. However, this simple recipe is an excellent chance to exercise your creativity. Experiment with different flavored syrups to see what suits your taste buds as a complement to delicious fresh mint and vodka. Ginger? Or even the more savory rosemary or sage? Perhaps a unique twist featuring local ingredients? The choices are endless!

<hr>

THE SWEET SMELL
OF TORTURE

Its sharp, peppery, mildly sour aroma and taste earned this plant the Latin name *Nasturtium officianale*—nose torture. But don't let that scare you off! Wild watercress is delicious. It also happens to be jam-packed with lots of vitamins and is a super-healthy green for the picking in much of Europe, Asia, and all over North America. I like combining it in the glass with the giddy-sweet tropical taste of fresh pineapple juice and a complementary dousing of tequila—a spirit that tends to have a vegetal, peppery note. ☞

Watercress

¼ cup (15g) wild watercress
1 ounce (30ml) pineapple juice
½ ounce (15ml) freshly squeezed lime juice
½ ounce (15ml) Cointreau
2 ounces (60ml) 100% blue agave reposado tequila
Pickled jalapeño or nasturtium leaf, for garnish

Drop the watercress into the bottom of a cocktail shaker, drizzle
in a little of the pineapple juice, and gently muddle. Fill the
cocktail shaker half-full with ice, and pour in the rest of the
pineapple juice, lime juice, Cointreau, and tequila. Shake for 25
to 30 seconds. Strain slowly into an ice-filled double rocks glass.
Garnish with a pickled jalapeño or nasturtium leaf.

Limes

STINGING NETTLE
SWIZZLE

———◆◆◆———

Take the bitter with the sweet—but don't get stung. Stinging nettles like to grow in moist, rich soil. And yes, the name is one to be heeded. Their stems are chock-a-block with spiny, sharp stickers that do not feel very nice when you brush up against them or, heaven forbid, grasp their hearty stalk with your bare hands. The ragged-looking leaves, too, have stickers but only on the tips and, to a less-sticky extent, around the perimeter of the leaf's edge. Use thick gloves to pick them. I use gloves plus a thick piece of canvas to grasp the stalk, which is edible, but I leave that to the true, tenacious foragers. It's the bitter leaves we're interested in here.

With Amari and other bitter sippers making such a surprising and yet very welcome showing in cocktail culture these days, it seemed fun to find another bittering source to balance the flavor spectrum in a cocktail like the swizzle. Instead of sugar, I use agave syrup because of its earthier, complementary flavor. It's best to pick nettles on the early side of spring, when the stickers are less sticky. Pluck off the leaves, and use kitchen shears to carefully snip off the spiny points. Then soak the leaves in a bowl of ice water to soften them up a little, while ensuring they're kept fresh before use. ☞

3–4 stinging nettle leaves, spines snipped and
gently washed, soaked, and patted dry

¾ ounce (22ml) agave syrup

2 ounces (60ml) aged rum

¾ ounce (22ml) freshly squeezed lime juice

1 wedge of lime, for garnish

Drop the nettle leaves in the bottom of a cocktail shaker, drizzle in a little of the agave syrup, and gently muddle. Fill the cocktail shaker half-full with ice, and pour in the rest of the agave syrup, rum, and lime juice. Shake for 25 to 30 seconds. Strain slowly into an ice-filled double rocks glass. Garnish with a lime wedge.

Nettles

RUE THE DAY

Carthusian monks were perennially secretive about the contents of Chartreuse, but I bet that there's some rue herb in there. Not only does the color reflect that spunky, acquired-taste of a liqueur, but its aroma and flavor embody the fresh, herbaceous nature for which it's known. It would be fun to try your hand at using rue in a Last Word (a drink that uses Chartreuse to great effect), but rue's lime-peel presence on the palate yearns for tequila. This drink was inspired by the Paloma, one of my favorite warm-weather drinks. 🖝

Rue

¼ cup (15g) rue herb
½ ounce (15ml) ginger syrup*
2–3 ounces (60–90ml) freshly squeezed pink grapefruit juice
2 ounces (60ml) 100% blue agave silver tequila
Club soda
1 peel of pink grapefruit, for garnish

Drop the rue into the bottom of a cocktail shaker, drizzle in a little of the ginger syrup, and gently muddle. Fill the cocktail shaker half-full with ice and pour in the rest of the ginger syrup, pink grapefruit juice, and tequila. Shake for 25 to 30 seconds. Strain slowly into an ice-filled Collins glass. Top with club soda and garnish with a pink grapefruit peel.

*Ginger Syrup
1 cup (200g) sugar
1 cup (235ml) water
1-inch (2.5-cm) nub of ginger, peeled and chopped

In a saucepot, simmer the sugar and water, stirring, until the sugar just starts to dissolve. Add the ginger. Simmer for 10 to 15 minutes. Allow to cool. Transfer to a sealed container, and refrigerate for up to a month.

NOTE: If you cannot find rue growing wild where you live, this lovely little plant can also be bought in seed packets and grown in your backyard or patio pots. However, if you are unable to source even the seeds, substitute rue for another savory herb. For the same citrusy flavor, why not try lemon verbena, cilantro (fresh coriander), or kaffir lime leaves.

FORAGER'S COCKTAILS

WILD DANDY

My husband Dan's Italian grandmother used to grab handfuls of these leaves from the yard as well as parks, wash them, and sautee them to make a garlicky, delicious side dish. Smart lady. Their mildly bitter, bright flavor goes great with tequila, too. Be careful of where you pick these, though—most parks use some kind of pesticide to keep critters at bay, and in many yards weedkiller often is employed to keep the feisty dandelion down. Always make sure you wash your leaves and flowers thoroughly, giving them a good cold-water soak, and then rinse a few more times after that. ☞

Dandelions

2 dandelion leaves, roughly torn
¼ ounce (7ml) ginger syrup*
2 ounces (60ml) 100% blue agave reposado tequila
1 ounce (30ml) freshly squeezed orange juice
Dandelion leaves and orange, for garnish

Drop the clean, torn dandelion leaves into a cocktail shaker. Pour in the ginger syrup and muddle, pressing on the leaves until they begin to break down slightly. Pour in the tequila and orange juice. Shake for 25 to 30 seconds. Slowly strain into an ice-filled double rocks glass. Using a standard vegetable peeler, gently slice only the skin of the orange peel (avoiding the bitter pith) above the drink, and drop the peel into the glass—dandelion leaves or an orange slice can also be added for garnish.

*Ginger Syrup
1 cup (200g) sugar
1 cup (235ml) water
1-inch (2.5-cm) nub of ginger, peeled and chopped

In a saucepot, simmer the sugar and water, stirring, until the sugar just starts to dissolve. Add the ginger. Simmer for 10 to 15 minutes. Allow to cool. Transfer to a sealed container, and refrigerate for up to a month.

SUMMER

Years ago, I wrote a weekly cocktail column for my local paper. I began by writing about the classics, but as the weather warmed and my local greenmarket opened, I found myself no less than thoroughly excited about spending a Saturday morning scouring fresh, colorful produce plucked by the farmers who drove from north, south, east, and west to bring their wares to enthusiastic (although occasionally stumped) city folk. I had two rules for myself on those farmers' market mornings: 1) I could buy only what I could haul back up the hill to my home (believe me, this was and still is a very good rule, as I tend to want far more than I could ever possibly ingest), and 2) I had to buy at least one item I'd never heard of, tried, or prepared before. A weekly produce challenge, if you will. Sometimes those items wound up not only inspiring a meal or a side dish but often a brand-new cocktail or an ingredient swap-out in a classic drink for my column. It gave me a whole new outlet for using (and using up) ingredients that I was feeling a little shy about trying. I hope these recipes get you excited to do the same.

HOPS & CROPS

For some of us, a pot on a stoop or a fire escape is about as wild as we can get, and you know what? There's nothing wrong with that. Foraging from your windowsill can be a satisfying experience, too. My nose discovered lemon verbena (*Aloysia citrodora*) before I laid eyes on its frondy abundance. And if you've ever brushed by it, you'll know what I mean. Its lemony, gum-like smell is so prominent and lovely, it's as if someone from the perfume counter just misted you as you walked by—but you actually liked it.

This flowering plant hails from South America, but like many popular rooted examples of modern horticulture, we managed to import and adapt it. It was first brought to Europe by Spanish and Portuguese merchant-explorers in the 1600s. My first plant was a wee spike in a tiny pot, but it grew quite quickly into a very big monster, stretching and climbing up to 3 feet high. (It probably would've grown much bigger had I not sequestered it to a container—you can plant it in the ground, too.) One of my favorite uses for the plant is another riff on the shandy, as with sheep sorrel. Here in the United States, the craft beer movement is blooming—and, as an outcropping, so to speak, regional hops and grain growing, too—with no signs of slowing down. Many of the craft brewers I like tend to tip heavily on the hops, making for some lip-smackingly bitter IPAs and intense double IPA brews. Adding a little lemony-sweet verbena syrup makes for an incredibly refreshing summertime quaff. 🐾

Juice of 1 lemon wedge
1 ounce (15ml) lemon-verbena syrup*
14-ounce (415ml) bottle of Imperial Pale Ale
1 fresh sprig of lemon verbena, for garnish

Squeeze the lemon juice into a pilsner glass. Add the syrup, and pour in the beer. Garnish with a sprig of lemon verbena as well as an optional lemon wedge.

*Lemon Verbena Syrup
¾ cup (150g) sugar
1 cup (235ml) water
1 handful of fresh lemon verbena leaves, gently rinsed

In a small pot, combine the lemon verbena leaves with the sugar and water. Cook over medium heat for about 10 minutes, stirring occasionally, until the sugar dissolves and the lemon verbena releases its oils and is fragrant. Allow to cool. Keep for up to a month in a sealed jar in the refrigerator.

ELDERFLOWER COOLER

The elderflower, like lots of fruits that begin with flora, is the start of the eventual elderberry (aka, *sambucus*—yup, it's in Sambuca, too). Like the best combo of vanilla beans and lilies, it has a pretty hypnotic aroma, and you don't have to wait for the fruit to enjoy it. You can pluck the blossoms and start using them as soon as they begin to bloom in the early summer. The small, white, multi-petaled flowers have a lovely lacy appearance that look great in a vase in your home, but they also taste pretty wonderful in this refreshing summer sipper. ☞

Elderflower

¾ ounce (22ml) elderflower syrup*
2 ounces (60ml) vodka
1 ounce (30ml) freshly squeezed grapefruit juice
2 ounces (60ml) club soda
1 sprig of elderflower (and slice of grapefruit if desired), for garnish

Pour all the ingredients into an ice-filled Collins glass. Stir, and garnish with a sprig of elderflower.

*Elderflower Syrup
2 cups (roughly 200g) elderflowers, gently rinsed
1 peel of grapefruit
2 cups (475ml) boiling water
1 cup (200g) sugar

Place the flowers and peel in a heatproof bowl, and pour over the boiling water. Cover the bowl, and allow to sit for at least six hours, preferably overnight. Strain out the flowers, and pour the liquid into a saucepan with the sugar and grapefruit peel. Heat to a simmer, stirring, until the sugar has dissolved. Keep in a sealed glass jar in the refrigerator for up to a month.

BEACH PLUM FIZZ

When I was a kid, all my friends' moms would harvest beach plums—sweet-tart little fruits—from the beach-rimming spots of my hometown in eastern Long Island. As I got older, I forgot about them, until a genius distiller named Steven DeAngelo shared a similar memory of stalking the wild beach plum as a kid along the sandy shores of Far Rockaway, Queens. DeAngelo, a fan of sloe gin, started a distillery called Greenhook Ginsmiths in Williamsburg, Brooklyn. When he realized that he couldn't get his hands on sloe fruits or English damson plums, his memory of childhood foraging kicked in: beach plums! Today, he makes a beautiful liqueur with these wild fruits. If you can't find his liqueur where you live, this is my attempt at putting my own childhood memories to good grown-up use.

Beach plums ripen during the last gasps of summer. Wash and pit them (they have a fairly big pit similar to that of a cherry, so employ a pitting device to rid yourself of it sooner rather than later). Then simply toss them in the freezer in freezerproof containers or sealable plastic bags so you can enjoy them all year long. In the meantime, a sweet-tart beach plum syrup is a great cocktail accompaniment. I like Plymouth gin for this recipe because it's a little bit softer in nature than a typical tarted-up London dry style. ☛

2 ounces (60ml) Plymouth gin
1 ounce (30ml) beach plum syrup*
½ ounce (15ml) freshly squeezed lemon juice
3–4 ounces (90–120ml) club soda
1 peel of lemon, for garnish

Fill a cocktail shaker half-full with ice cubes, pour in the gin, beach plum syrup, and lemon juice. Shake for 20 to 35 seconds. Slowly strain into an ice-filled Collins glass. Top with club soda, and garnish with a lemon peel.

*Beach Plum Syrup
1 cup (225g) beach plums, washed and pitted
1 cup (200g) sugar
¼ cup (60ml) water

Combine the plums, sugar, and water in a saucepot. Simmer over medium heat, stirring for about 15 to 20 minutes, until the plums start to break down and the sugar dissolves. Allow to cool. Transfer to a sealed jar and keep for up to a month in the refrigerator.

NOTE: Should you not live in the vicinity of beach plums, you may want to reconsider some life choices. But in the meantime, try experimenting with tart damsons—or other plum varieties combined with some fresh cranberries—for your own individual sweet-tart twist.

SHEEP SORREL SHANDY

The word in the meadow is that sheep sorrel is so-called because it looks a little like its namesake. The long, main oblong leaf grows to a pointed tip, kind of like the long nose bridge of an adult sheep, and the two smaller, similarly shaped leaves that spring from the base resemble two cute little ears. Although this makes sheep sorrel pretty easy to pick from a lineup, it would be more apropos if it were shaped like a lemon—the leaves (and later-season flowers) have a deliciously sour taste, which is why it's fun to use them for a version of that ultimately refreshing summer sipper, a shandy. 👉

Sheep sorrel

1 ounce (30ml) sheep sorrel and lemon syrup*
14 ounces (415ml) saison-style beer

Pour the syrup into a pilsner glass. Top with saison-style beer.

*Sheep Sorrel and Lemon Syrup
1½ cups (300g) sugar
1½ cups (355ml) water
1 cup (roughly 100g) sheep sorrel leaves, washed
Peel from 1 lemon

Combine the sugar and water in a saucepot over medium heat. Stir until the sugar begins to dissolve. Drop in the sheep sorrel leaves and lemon peel, and cook on a low simmer for 15 minutes. Allow to cool. Strain out the leaves and lemon peel. Transfer to a sealed container or jar, and store in the refrigerator for up to one month.

———◆◦◆———

ORCHARD
OLD-FASHIONED

———◦•◦•———

One of the things I love about the Old-Fashioned is that it has a little bit of not-so-old-fashioned versatility that belies its name. Although many a fine bartender has taken to eschewing the 1970s and 1980s fruit-bowl additions to the drink (such as the famed muddled orange and cherry), if there's fresh fruit around, I like to go for it and toss 'em back in the mix. So swap out that orange and cherry for whatever you like. Purists may damn such unbridled behavior, but as we're not curing cancer here, it's A-OK to color outside the lines a little bit. Peaches seem like a natural fit (and to that effect, I also switch the traditional rye in this drink to bourbon). And despite the fact that I do not live in the great state of Georgia, small, sweet versions of these peaches seem to grow everywhere from craggy branches around where I live. I can't find enough things to do with them in the summer. I make jam, preserve wedges of them in syrup, grill them, cook with them, and, of course, cocktails are on the docket, too. Their juicy, sweet flavor gets a nice complement from bourbon whiskey, and to it I like to add some fresh, bright lemon thyme from the pots in my backyard. ☛

1 sugar cube
3 dashes of peach bitters
1 peach, skinned, pitted, and cut into wedges
3 sprigs of lemon thyme
2½ ounces (75ml) bourbon
Slices of peach, for garnish

Drop a sugar cube into a rocks glass. Drip 3 dashes of peach bitters onto it, and add the peach wedges and two of the thyme sprigs. Using a muddler or wooden spoon, muddle all the ingredients together while crushing the cube. Remove the thyme sprig. Add 4 to 5 ice cubes, and pour the bourbon over the top. Stir, and garnish with the remaining thyme sprig or slices of peach.

WILD STRAWBERRY MARGARITA

———◆•◆•◆———

My friend Shawn Kelley throws just about the best summer parties of anyone I know. Each summer, her narrow Brooklyn backyard fills with the aromas of myriad slow-cooked meats and throngs shoulder to shoulder with friends and colleagues from different parts of the spirits biz—writers, distillers, bartenders, and historians. It makes for a pretty interesting bowl of punch. One year, my friend St. John Frizell, a writer, bartender, and owner of the wonderful Fort Defiance in Red Hook, brought a big jar full of deliciously bright red liquid. What was it? Tequila that had had strawberries soaking in it for a good week in his fridge. It tasted like boozy, berry heaven.

I'm a big proponent of avoiding certain things until they're in season, if only because the flavor is the Technicolor version of the washed-out, insipid cultivated versions. Not to mention the indulgence of using fossil fuel to ship things that need not be shipped. But that's a soapbox for another time—right now, we're going to talk about wild strawberries. They are smaller than your average, cultivated version, with a white flower and a sweet, concentrated flavor that can't be beat. Nab 'em before the birds do. ☞

2 ounces (60ml) strawberry tequila*
1 ounce (30ml) Cointreau
¾ ounce (22ml) freshly squeezed lime juice
1 wild strawberry, for garnish

Fill a cocktail shaker half-full with ice cubes, pour in the tequila, Cointreau, and lime juice. Shake for 20 to 35 seconds. Slowly strain into an ice-filled ball jar and garnish with a fresh wild strawberry.

*Strawberry Tequila

1 pint (500g) fresh wild strawberries, rinsed, hulled, and cut in half
750ml bottle 100% blue agave silver tequila

Add the strawberries to a large, sealable glass jar. Pour in the tequila, seal, and place in a cool, dark place for at least two days and up to a week. Strain out the strawberries, transfer the liquid to a clean sealed bottle, and keep the tequila indefinitely in the refrigerator.

TIP: After straining out the strawberries, the color will have leached out of them, and they won't be as pretty. Don't toss them, though! Use them along with some fresh ones to make tequila-strawberry ice cream or jam. Yum.

LET LOVAGE RULE

You have mild-mannered Bruce Banner, and then you have his alter ego, the Hulk. This isn't a bad way to think about *Levisticum officinale*, or lovage (in my humble opinion, the best, most-fun-to-say herb name ever). While celery is distinct, it's pretty mild in flavor and gets to be about a foot long at its usual supermarket-sold max. But lovage? Oh boy. Its flavor is like celery on steroids, and one little plant can soar up to 8 feet. Seriously. And it's perennial! If you think about it, it's a pretty selfless plant. Lovage is a great guest in the garden, and with a botanical-bursting spirit like gin? It's a shoo-in. Try it in a classic Bloody Mary, too, for an extra herby kick. ☞

Lovage

6 lovage leaves, washed
1 ounce (30ml) basil-mint syrup*
2 ounces (60ml) London dry gin
1 ounce (30ml) freshly squeezed lemon juice
3 ounces (90ml) club soda
Mixed leaves or lemon, for garnish

Drop the lovage leaves into a cocktail shaker. Drizzle in a little of the syrup, and gently muddle. Fill the cocktail shaker half-full with ice, and pour in the rest of the syrup, gin, and lemon juice. Shake for 25 to 30 seconds. Strain into an ice-filled Collins glass and top with club soda. If desired, garnish with mint, lovage, or basil leaves and lemon.

*Basil-Mint Syrup
1 cup (40g) basil and mint leaves, combined (½ cup of each)
¾ cup (150g) sugar
1 cup (235ml) water

Drop the basil and mint leaves into a saucepot. Muddle gently and briefly. Add in the sugar and water, and simmer over medium heat, stirring, until the sugar dissolves. Allow to cool. Strain out the leaves, transfer to a sealed container, and refrigerate for up to a month.

———◆◆◆———

TAMAR'S WILD BLUEBERRY DAIQUIRI

I owe a lot to my very dear friend Tamar Smith. Not only does she fully receive credit for getting my husband and me together (a story that involves a ballet dancer, a coup, a broken heart, and a nor'easter, exactly in that order). She also schooled me on folk and blues, was part and parcel to my first, real grown-up apartment, and took me on the hike in the Adirondack Mountains where I had my very first wild blueberry. They were scrappy and a little scrawny in comparison to the ones I knew from the supermarket, but sitting on a mountaintop overlooking the Hudson Valley, no less delicious. I think probably more so. Blueberries are native to North America, and these antioxidant-rich little orbs actually began their commercial entry into the fold as a form of sustenance for the Union Army during the Civil War. ☞

Blueberries

¼ cup (35g) wild blueberries (non-wild blueberries,
while less fun, can also be used)
½ ounce (15ml) simple syrup*
2 ounces (60ml) white rum
1 ounce (30ml) freshly squeezed lime juice
1 peel of lime, for garnish

Put the blueberries in a cocktail shaker, and gently muddle. Fill the shaker half-full with ice, and pour in the simple syrup, rum, and lime juice. Shake for 25 to 30 seconds. Slowly strain into an ice-filled double rocks glass. Garnish with the lime peel.

*Simple Syrup
¾ cup (150g) sugar
1 cup (235ml) water

In a saucepot, gently simmer the sugar and water over medium heat for about 5 minutes, stirring, until the sugar dissolves. Allow to cool. Transfer to a sealed container, and refrigerate for up to a month.

THE CONCORD

———◦◆◦———

Concord grapes are considered something between *Vitis labrusca*—that is, grapes native to the Americas—and a cultivated final product of a clever farmer in Concord, Massachusetts. In 1849, Ephraim Wales Bull used native grapes growing on his farm to tease out these juicy, plump cultivars that have since become the source of everything from jam to juice. You see them not only at farmers' markets but often in back gardens, both urban and rural, creeping over trellises that groan under the ripened weight of the hanging bunches. In North America, they are, in effect, everywhere.

It was mid-autumn, and quart-sized paper containers overflowed with the pretty, purply orbs. I snatched up two and brought them home. But instead of dragging out the big pot for making preserves, I decided to whip up a cocktail worthy of a Saturday night. I rinsed the grapes, plucked one, and popped it in my mouth. Despite the skin being slightly thicker than your typical table grape and having gigantic seeds, they were bright and juicy—almost syrupy. One word came to mind: rye. The sweet, concentrated flavor of the grapes with the spiked, spicy kick of whiskey would be perfect.

I did a little digging and found inspiration in the classic cocktail the Allegheny—a combination of bourbon, blackberry brandy, dry vermouth, a bit of lemon juice, and bitters. I liked the idea of swapping out bourbon for rye and the blackberry brandy for Concord syrup. (This would, in effect, lower the alcohol content of the drink, making having more than one a no-brainer instead of leaving me feeling like I had no brain.)

The lemon juice was the perfect foil to knit together the sweet syrup and the spicy rye.

The name of this drink might seem obvious, but, like those juicy grapes, there's more to it than meets the eye. It's a nod to the cocktail's origins and how it took flight—the Concorde, one of the most powerful planes to make a trans-Atlantic trek, and Allegheny Airlines, a now-defunct plane operator based out of Pittsburgh, Pennsylvania. 🖛

Concord grapes

1½ ounces (45ml) rye
1 ounce (30ml) dry vermouth
½ ounce (15ml) Concord grape syrup
½ ounce (15ml) freshly squeezed lemon juice
2 dashes of fig bitters
1 lemon twist, for garnish

Fill a cocktail shaker half-full with ice cubes. Add all the ingredients, and shake for 25 to 30 seconds. Strain into a coupe glass, and garnish with the lemon twist.

*Concord Grape Syrup

1 quart (1 liter) Concord grapes, destemmed

Heat the grapes in a medium pot over medium-low heat for 6 to 7 minutes, or until their skins crack and the grapes cook down enough to release their juice. Remove from the heat, and allow to cool. Set a fine mesh sieve over a bowl and press the cooled grapes through to extract all the juice. Store in an airtight container in the refrigerator for up to one month or freeze for up to several months for future use.

NOTE: If you do not live in a Concord-growing region, here's a simple and no-less-tasty alternative. In place of the grapes, pick a slightly larger portion of wild blackberries. Follow the same method for washing, heating, and pressing, but as blackberries are a little more tart, add in ½ cup of sugar and ½ cup of water. Simmer, and stir until the sugar has completely dissolved. Press through a sieve, and discard the solids. Store as with the Concord grape syrup.

———◆●◆———

WILD MINT MOJITO

A friend recently told me that not only does he like mint, he almost encourages it to grow so out of control that it basically takes over his entire lawn. That way, when he mows, the whole place smells like one, big, beautiful Mojito. Few drinks have taken the world by storm as much as the Mojito, and I can think of no better use for snatching up handfuls of the herb and using it with wild abandon. In the summer, the smell of mint is almost like herby air-conditioning, cooling you off with just one whiff. Wild mint, or *Mentha arvensis*, like its other green-leafy brethren, grows with abandon, too. It was a popular remedy for everything from stomach maladies to colds among Native Americans—and it still is. But to heal what ails you after a long, hard week at the office? A Wild Mint Mojito is just the thing. ☛

Mint

7–8 fresh wild mint leaves, rinsed and patted dry
1 lime, rinsed, dried, and cut into quarters
1 ounce (30ml) mint syrup*
2 ounces (60ml) white rum
3–4 ounces (90–120ml) club soda
1 sprig of fresh mint, for garnish

Drop the mint leaves and lime quarters into a Collins glass, and muddle. Fill with crushed ice. Add the mint syrup, rum, and club soda. Stir, and garnish with a mint sprig.

*Mint Syrup
1 cup (40g) mint leaves
1 cup (200g) sugar
1 cup (235ml) water

Drop the mint leaves into a saucepot. Briefly muddle them, pressing on the leaves until they begin to break down slightly. Add the sugar and water, and simmer over medium heat, stirring, until the sugar dissolves. Allow to cool. Strain out the leaves, transfer to a sealed container, and refrigerate for up to a month.

VALENTINE

When I was a kid, my mom used to buy me Caswell–Massey glycerin rose soap. I loved the stuff. I loved it so much, in fact, that I wouldn't use it to bathe but to make my clothing drawers smell like rose petals had been showered all over them. Because, really, there is nothing so beautiful as the smell of rose petals. I have a couple of rose bushes in my backyard, which, for years, I simultaneously admired and ignored. It turns out that is a good thing—wild roses don't like to be fussed over too much.

Wild roses look a bit different than your average Valentine rose in that they have fewer petals and don't form in the tight, multi-petaled blossom as cultivated roses do. Instead, they almost let it all hang out. Pluck their petals to make the most gorgeously scented simple syrup known to humankind. ☛

Wild rose

2 ounces (60ml) vodka
¾ ounce (22ml) rose petal syrup
1 ounce (30ml) lemon juice
1–2 rose petals (or a whole rose), for garnish

In a cocktail shaker half-full with ice, pour in the vodka, rose petal syrup, and lemon juice. Shake for 25 to 30 seconds. Slowly strain into a coupe glass. Garnish with rose petals or a whole rose.

*Rose Petal Syrup
1 cup (235ml) water
¾ cup (150g) sugar
1 cup (80g) wild or garden rose petals, gently rinsed and dried

Combine the water and sugar in a saucepan over medium heat, stirring until the sugar just begins to dissolve. Add the rose petals, and simmer for 10 minutes, stirring, until the sugar completely dissolves and the color leaches from the petals. Transfer to a jar with a tight lid, and store in the refrigerator for up to a month.

EATS, FRUITS & LEAVES

I discovered alache where I find a lot of things new to me—my local seasonal greenmarket. It was early summer, and I was buying more wild strawberries than a person has a right to have. As I was paying, I noticed a humble little posy of green leaves with pretty purple flowers sitting with its snipped, gathered stems in a shallow tub of water. "What's that?" I asked the farmer, as she handed me my change. "Alache," she answered. "You can eat it raw, cook it, do whatever." Its lonely little perch made me pick it up, pay for it, and stuff it in my bag, fearful that some alache-loving lurker might sweep up behind me and nab this new green before I could get my head around what to do with it. Late spring or early summer is the best time for this plant from the Malvaceae family (which also includes everything from okra to cotton—who knew?). This is when the tender leaves have a soft, vegetal flavor. They seemed a natural fit with a little agave and soft, richly flavored, oval-shaped Italian plums. ☛

Alache, or anoda cristata

4–5 alache leaves, washed and roughly torn
1 Italian plum, skinned, pitted, and cut into wedges
(or any fresh plum you fancy)
¾ ounce (22ml) agave syrup
2 ounces (60ml) silver rum
2 drops of Angostura bitters

Drop the alache leaves into a cocktail shaker along with the plum wedges. Gently muddle. Fill the cocktail shaker half-full with ice, and pour in the syrup, rum, and bitters. Shake for 25 to 30 seconds. Strain into a cocktail or coupe glass. Garnish with an optional alache flower.

NOTE: Alache is commonly known as anoda cristata, or crested anoda. It can be found throughout the Americas and Australia and as an introduced plant in other regions.

———◆◆◆———

MULBERRY SMASH

Morus rubra is the species of sweet-tart mulberries that grows in my neck of the woods. They are both blackish-purple and red and a little longer than your typical blackberry. Mulberries grow on trees all over the city where I live, and if the birds don't nab them or they aren't staining the sidewalks, they are truly some of the best low-hanging fruit you can easily find right in your very own neighborhood or park.

As with any fruit, herb, or green you gather, rinse your berries thoroughly—but not until you're ready to use them. After rinsing, they will never fully dry, and that tends to speed up the rotting process in the refrigerator. Wash them as you use them, allow to dry, and then by all means make this smash. ☞

Mulberries

4–5 fresh mulberries, rinsed
2 peels of lemon
3 mint leaves
¾ ounce (22ml) simple syrup*
2 ounces (60ml) bourbon

Drop the mulberries, 1 lemon peel, and the mint leaves into a cocktail shaker. Gently muddle. Fill the cocktail shaker half-full with ice and pour in the simple syrup and bourbon. Shake for 25 to 30 seconds. Strain into an ice-filled double rocks glass or ball jar. Garnish with the remaining lemon peel or a lemon slice and additional optional mint leaves.

*Simple Syrup
¾ cup (150g) sugar
1 cup (235ml) water

In a saucepot, gently simmer the sugar and water over medium heat for about 5 minutes, stirring, until the sugar dissolves. Allow to cool. Transfer to a sealed container, and refrigerate for up to a month.

I'M YOUR HUCKLEBERRY

Flips are generally thought of as holiday drinks—it's got a whole egg in it, what could be more rich? But adding fresh fruit, a lighter spirit like gin, as well as the herby notes of both the rosemary and the Campari will brighten up your standard flip. In New York, the huckleberry goes by the name of *Gaylussacia baccata*, and it looks a lot like a blueberry (which you can certainly use as a substitute here). They grow on shrubs in the craggiest of craggy spots, favoring rocky, dry soil—so if you're hot for huckleberries, a nice nature hike is in your near future.

4–5 huckleberries
2 ounces (60ml) London dry gin
1 whole egg
¾ ounce (22ml) rosemary syrup*
½ ounce (15ml) Campari
1 sprig of rosemary, for garnish (optional)

Add all the ingredients to a cocktail shaker, reserving 1 huckleberry. Shake vigorously for 25 to 30 seconds. Add ice, and shake for 20 more seconds. Strain into a coupe glass. Garnish with the reserved huckleberry or a sprig of rosemary.

*Rosemary Syrup

3–4 sprigs of rosemary

¾ cup (150g) sugar

1 cup (235ml) water

Drop the rosemary into a saucepot. Muddle gently and briefly. Add the sugar and water, and simmer over medium heat, stirring, until the sugar dissolves. Allow to cool. Transfer to a sealed container, and refrigerate for up to a month.

FALL

No matter how old I get, the school-time smell of snappy, dry leaves and pencil lead makes me feel like everything's new and starting over. But this is a little at odds with what's happening all around—the last gasp of tomatoes and other fruit overflow bins at roadside stands and greenmarket tables; plants begin to put energy back into their roots; daylight gets shorter and shorter. But I'm still more attuned to that back-to-school sensibility: what can I learn right now? How can I set myself up for a fall full of great cocktails?

Fall is possibly one of the best times of year to use what's around you to plan for the cold days ahead—be it simmering up a root-vegetable shrub (which you can sip without the booze, too—a little club soda and ice make a refreshing afternoon "-ade" to sip on) or challenging yourself to collect a stinky pile of ginkgo nuts. It's the season that, apropos of its name, makes you fall in love with the kitchen all over again.

CAPED CRUSADER

Shrubby cranberry bushes like to grow in moist spots, and places like Massachusetts and New Jersey have become famed for their cultivated versions of these fruits, which show up on supermarket shelves. They are delicious, but the wild kind, *Vaccinium macrocarpon*, are fun to seek when you're out exploring on sunny fall weekends. The leaves look a little like a darker version of the rue leaves we were mixing up drinks with back in spring, and they start off in that season with an exotic-looking flower (that looks awfully nice in a vase, too). If you're going cranberry hunting, wear pants that you don't mind getting a bit mucky, and be sure to bring along extra sealable plastic bags. Just like the store-bought version, wild cranberries can be frozen and saved. ☞

Cranberries

2 ounces (60ml) bourbon
½ ounce (15ml) Oloroso sherry
½ ounce (15ml) cranberry-rosemary-orange syrup*
1 sprig of rosemary, for garnish

Fill a cocktail shaker half-full with ice cubes. Pour in the bourbon, sherry, and syrup. Shake for 25 to 30 seconds. Slowly strain into an ice-filled rocks glass, and garnish with a small sprig of rosemary.

*Cranberry-Rosemary-Orange Syrup
1 cup (200g) sugar
1 cup (235ml) water
2 cups wild cranberries, rinsed and chopped
2–3 wide orange peels
2 sprigs of rosemary

In a saucepot, simmer the sugar and water, stirring, until the sugar starts to dissolve. Add the cranberries, orange peel, and rosemary and simmer for 10 to 15 minutes. Strain out the liquid, discard the solids, and store in an airtight jar in the refrigerator for up to a month.

NOTE: If you live outside of the select cranberry-growing regions, these delightful berries can also be foraged elsewhere—in specialty supermarkets around the world, often in the freezer section. Cranberries are delicate little things and not the heartiest of travelers.

SLEEPY TIME TIPPLE

Chamomile tea is everywhere—no shortage of that on the shelves. But fresh chamomile flowers? They make your house smell amazingly lovely when they bloom in the spring, and they are so crazy prolific in the way they grow that you can harvest armsful and make your own tea for the upcoming months. You can also take the flowers and make the most delicious, everlasting, simple spirit infusion. Genever is where gin began, both stylistically (it's a heftier, maltier, headier version) and geographically (Holland). Eventually, it was co-opted by the Brits and became what we know as gin today. A good way to think of it: gin is to genever what Kate Moss is to Christina Hendricks. Think on that while sipping this. ☞

Chamomile

2 ounces (60ml) chamomile-infused genever*
¾ ounce (22ml) freshly squeezed lemon juice
½ ounce (15ml) lemon syrup*
1 sprig of chamomile flowers or lemon twist, for garnish

Fill a cocktail shaker half-full with ice cubes. Pour in the chamomile-infused genever, lemon juice, and syrup. Shake for 25 to 30 seconds. Strain slowly into a cocktail or coupe glass. Garnish with a sprig of fresh chamomile (when in season) or a lemon twist (when not).

*Chamomile-Infused Genever
1 cup (roughly 100g) fresh chamomile flowers, rinsed,
dried, trimmed from stems
750ml bottle genever

Put the flowers in a quart-sized (1-liter) sealable jar. Pour in the genever. Allow to sit for 24 to 48 hours (depending on how floral you want your infusion to taste). Strain, and store indefinitely.

*Lemon Syrup
1 cup (200g) sugar
1 cup (235ml) water
2–3 wide lemon peels

In a saucepot, simmer the sugar and water, stirring, until the sugar starts to dissolve. Add the lemon peels, and simmer for 10 to 15 minutes. Store in an airtight jar in the refrigerator for up to a month.

DIETSCH ME THIS

Michael Dietsch wrote *Shrubs*, an awesome book all about that vinegar-based "-ade" that not only refreshes with its sweet-tart nature but is also a great way of preserving everything from strawberries to peaches. Years ago Michael vetted a cocktail book I was writing after the bartender I'd hired to do it left me in the lurch. Good man, that Michael Dietsch. So at the very least, I owe him a cocktail in his name. Humbly taking a cue from his great book and the wonderful notion of preserving the season in a shrub, this one makes good use of rose hips—those nubby, little mini-apple-like bits left on your bushes after the petals fall off. Get them before the deer do to make this beet-rose hip sipper. ☞

Beets

2 ounces (60ml) vodka
2 tablespoons (30ml) beet-rose hip shrub*
3–4 ounces (90–120ml) club soda
Optional beet leaves, for garnish

Pour the vodka and shrub into an ice-filled Collins glass. Stir, and top with club soda.

*Beet-Rose Hip Shrub
3 beets, peeled and roughly chopped
1 cup (120g) rose hips, rinsed and roughly chopped
¾ cup (175ml) cider vinegar
2 ounces (60ml) white wine vinegar
1 cup (200g) sugar

Juice your beets and rose hips, or combine them in a blender or food processer until smooth and press through a mesh sieve or cheesecloth to separate the juice from the remaining chunky bits. Combine all the ingredients in a quart-sized (1-liter) sealable jar, and refrigerate overnight. The next day, give the contents a good shake, and let them sit for one more day. Take the jar out of the fridge, strain once more, and keep your shrub in the refrigerator in a sealed jar for as long as you like.

GINKGO ALEXANDER

I learned about the wonders of the ginkgo nut when I was an editor at *Edible Manhattan*. My friend, cookbook author Raquel Pelzel, wrote a story on chef Matt Weingarten and his fondness for foraging these nuts in city parks. The idea thoroughly fascinated me. It never in a million years occurred to me to do anything except run quickly past the smelly, discarded piles of gingko fruit on the trails in my local park. Bring them home? Are you crazy? Well ... maybe not. You can identify the chestnut-like durian, as it is also known, by the shape of the leaves. (They look like a pretty souvenir fan from the South Pacific.) They smell a lot like cheese rind—or old, sweaty socks, depending on how much you like stinky stuff. But look past this. Roast them for my take on a Brandy Alexander. Since you really need only one for the garnish here, salt the extras, and snack on them while you sip this cocktail. ☞

Gingko nuts

2 ounces (60ml) brandy
1 ounce (30ml) crème de cacao
½ ounce (30ml) half and half
1 ginkgo nut, roasted, for garnish*

Fill a cocktail shaker half-full with ice cubes. Pour in the brandy, crème de cacao, and half and half. Shake for 25 to 30 seconds. Strain slowly into a cocktail or coupe glass. Hold the roasted ginkgo nut over the glass, and grate it over to garnish.

*Roasted Ginkgo Nuts

Preheat the oven to 325°F (165°C). Rinse off the sticky outside flesh, and allow to dry thoroughly. Spread the nuts on a pan, and roast them for about 20 to 25 minutes. With a mallet or the wide part of a butcher knife, gently crack off the outer shell, and discard it.

NOTE: If you live somewhere without wild ginkgo nuts—which is most likely also a place without half and half cartons in every grocery store—try foraging in your local specialty food or health food store. For that elusive half and half, you can make your own by mixing one part milk to one part single cream.

SPICE & ICE

The first time I heard about wild ginger was when a nursery recommended it as groundcover for a shady spot in my garden. Honestly, I never considered it beyond that until a young, forage-loving chef told me he'd been rummaging through the woods for wild ginger over the weekend. As it turns out, the rhizome base of this plant offers a more delicate bite than the knobby versions we find in stores. I love making syrup with the rhizomes and combining it with spicy rye whiskey. 🖝

Wild ginger leaves

2 ounces (60ml) rye
½ ounce (15ml) wild ginger syrup*
3–4 ounces (90–120ml) club soda
Candied ginger, for garnish

Pour the rye, syrup, and club soda into an ice-filled Collins glass. Stir, and garnish with a piece of candied ginger or optional fresh ginger slices.

*Wild Ginger Syrup
1 cup (200g) sugar
1 cup (235ml) water
½ cup wild ginger rhizomes, washed and chopped

In a saucepot, simmer the sugar and water, stirring, until the sugar starts to dissolve. Add the ginger, and simmer for 10 to 15 minutes. Store in an airtight jar in the refrigerator for up to a month.

BASIL-ELDERBERRY COCKTAIL

Elderberries begin to ripen in midsummer, but you can pick them all the way through to early autumn—right in time for cold and flu season. According to botanical and medicinal lore, the little black berries are the cure for what ails you when the coughing and hacking season starts. Indeed, they are vitamin-packed. But when cooked down into a syrup, elderberries make a lovely addition to sauces, glazes, and cocktails. I like to add a little peppercorn-kick to mine and, here, make use of late-season basil, too. ☞

Elderberries

3–4 basil leaves, plus extra for optional garnish
2 ounces (60ml) vodka
1 ounce (30ml) elderberry syrup*
¾ ounce (22ml) freshly squeezed lime juice

Drop the basil leaves into a cocktail shaker, and gently muddle. Half-fill with ice cubes, and pour in the vodka, syrup, and lime juice. Shake for 25 to 30 seconds. Strain into a cocktail glass. If desired, garnish with basil leaves.

*Elderberry Syrup
1 pound (455g) elderberries, destemmed and rinsed
1 cup (200g) sugar
½ cup (120ml) water
1 teaspoon black peppercorns

Place the elderberries in a saucepot. Briefly muddle to break the skins a bit. Add the sugar, water, and peppercorns. Simmer over medium heat until the berries have broken down thoroughly and you have a nice, thick, dark syrup. Strain through a fine mesh sieve, and discard any leftover solids. Store in a sealed jar in the refrigerator for up to a month.

WOOD SORREL SOUR

Wood sorrel looks so much like clover that you might have been looking at this prolific grower for years and not realized you had an abundant source of really delicious tea at your feet. What makes wood sorrel stand out from regular ol' green clover is that it has a wee flower that pops up here and there (in delicate soft shades of pink, purple, yellow, and white). The other thing about wood sorrel is that it's super lemony tasting. Pretty cool, right? Make tea from it and drink it all on its own, or make a new kind of "sour" by mixing it with bourbon. ☛

Wood sorrel

2 ounces (60ml) bourbon
1 ounce (30ml) wood sorrel tea*
1 tablespoon (15g) sugar
A few sprigs of wood sorrel or lemon peel, for garnish

Fill a cocktail shaker half-full with ice cubes. Pour in the bourbon, wood sorrel tea, and sugar. Shake for 20 seconds. Strain slowly into an ice-filled double rocks glass. Garnish with a few sprigs of wood sorrel or a lemon peel.

*Wood Sorrel Tea
1 cup (roughly 100g) wood sorrel, washed
2 cups (475ml) boiling water
4 ounces (120ml) simple syrup*

Place the wood sorrel in a heat-proof bowl. Pour the boiling water over it, and add the simple syrup. Allow to steep for 20 minutes.

*Simple Syrup
¾ cup (150g) sugar
1 cup (235ml) water

In a saucepot, gently simmer the sugar and water over medium heat for about 5 minutes, stirring, until the sugar dissolves. Allow to cool. Transfer to a sealed container, and refrigerate for up to a month.

DANDELION SMASH II

Dandelions keep on truckin' right into fall; but as the seasons progress, the flavor of this common weed changes, too. The leaves grow broader and even more bitter as time ticks on toward winter. I like how that flavor complements a spicy spirit like rye, playing up its savory nature. Balance it out with a little lemon syrup. ☛

Dandelions

2 dandelion leaves, washed, patted dry, and torn
¾ ounce (22ml) lemon syrup*
2 ounces (60ml) rye
1 broad lemon peel or slice, for garnish

Drop the dandelion leaves into a cocktail shaker, drizzle in a little of the lemon syrup, and muddle. Fill the shaker half-full with ice cubes. Pour in the rye and the rest of the syrup. Shake for 25 to 30 seconds. Strain slowly into an ice-filled double rocks glass, and garnish with a broad lemon peel or slice.

*Lemon Syrup
1 cup (200g) sugar
1 cup (235ml) water
2–3 wide lemon peels

In a saucepot, simmer the sugar and water, stirring, until the sugar starts to dissolve. Add the lemon peel, and simmer for 10 to 15 minutes. Store in an airtight jar in the refrigerator for up to a month.

SMARTY PANTS

Sage is one of my all-time favorite herbs. The smell of it! Oh man—it just makes me hungry. I also love how pretty its leaves are. Rub your thumb across its plush surface, and not only will you be rewarded with how utterly soft it is, but your fingers will smell delicious afterward, too. I plant a lot of *Salvia officinalis*, but then I'm left figuring out what do with my bumper crop when autumn comes. Using it in a cocktail like this adds a little savory herbiness that complements a spirit like gin nicely. ☞

Sage

3–4 sage leaves, rinsed and patted dry
½ ounce (15ml) freshly squeezed orange juice
2½ ounces (75ml) London dry gin
½ ounce (15ml) dry vermouth
1 broad orange peel and optional sage leaves, for garnish

Drop the sage leaves into a mixing glass, add a little of the fresh orange juice, and muddle, pressing on the leaves until they begin to break down slightly. Fill the glass half-full with ice cubes. Pour in the gin, vermouth, and the rest of the orange juice. Stir for 25 to 30 seconds. Strain slowly into a cocktail glass, and garnish with a broad orange peel and optional sage leaves.

MARY LIKES CARROTS

There's nothing like a really great Bloody Mary. But a Bloody Mary made with peak-season tomatoes? Sign me up. I'd always seen the requisite celery stalk in this classic cocktail, but on my first of many visits to New Orleans, I stumbled upon a little place called the Columns where that stalk was subbed for a pickled green bean. Since then, I like putting all sorts of pickled veggies in my Bloodys: beans, okra, and, in this case, carrots.

Separate the skin from your tomatoes by scoring them and dropping them into a pot of boiling water. When the skin starts to peel—likely no more than a minute—take them out, and run them under cold water, then peel the skin, and discard. Many recipes will tell you to get rid of the seeds—personally, I love 'em and leave 'em.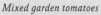

Mixed garden tomatoes

4–5 fresh mixed garden tomatoes, skinned
2 tablespoons (30g) horseradish
1 ounce (30ml) freshly squeezed lemon juice
1 teaspoon (5g) freshly ground white pepper
1 teaspoon (5g) sea salt
2 ounces (60ml) vodka
1 dash of hot sauce
2–3 pickled carrots*

Puree the skinned tomatoes, horseradish, lemon juice, white pepper, and salt in a blender. Pour the vodka into an ice-filled Collins glass. Top this with the tomato mixture and a dash of hot sauce and garnish with the pickled carrots.

*Pickled Carrots
1 pound (455g) carrots, preferably small and spindly,
trimmed to fit into a 1-quart (1-liter) glass mason jar
2 cups (475ml) water
1 cup (240ml) apple cider vinegar
½ cup (120ml) white wine vinegar
¼ cup (50g) sugar
2 tablespoons (30g) kosher salt
1 tablespoon (15g) fennel seed
1 bay leaf (fresh or dried, depending on your yard or cupboard)

In a pot, combine the carrots and water, and bring to a boil. Cook for 1 minute, then drain and run under cold water. Add the rest of the ingredients into the pot and simmer for about 5 minutes. Allow to cool. Arrange the carrots in the mason jar(s), and pour in the brining liquid. Refrigerate in the sealed jar for up to two months.

WINTER

— ❖ —

When I was a kid, I really used to like stories of seemingly impossible, mysterious, mildly scary secret doorways and tunnels discovered in unlikely spots, forces of good overcoming forces of evil, and creatures with rich inner lives. One of my favorites comes from *Aesop's Fables*: the indelible tale of "The Ant and the Grasshopper." That one has really stuck with me. Anytime I find myself being wasteful, a picture of a hopping, soon-to-be-regretful grasshopper pops up in my mind's eye. The older I get, the more I like the idea of being an ant that thinks ahead, saves, and stores. To me, that's the reward that awaits you in winter, from the plate (hello, last summer's frozen pesto!) to the cocktail glass (brandied Italian summer plums and cherries, please!). With a little planning and imagination, that reward can be a unique ingredient or garnish in every sip you take while the snow falls outside your window.

PEAR IT UP

My friend Tony DiDio always keeps a crate of apples or pears in the entryway of his Brooklyn brownstone. "Cold storage!" he told me when I asked what was up with all the fruit in his foyer. Indeed, the cool climes of his entryway made a pretty good spot to keep these orchard fruits in good shape (not to mention a convenient spot for grabbing a healthy snack on the way out the door). I love pears and apples all fall and winter long, and I use them in main courses, salads, side dishes, and (of course) baked goods because they make the house smell great. They also make a lovely addition to sparkling wine that is a little like sparkling hard cider. Pears and ginger are such a natural fit; use this syrup on pound cake or ice cream, too! ☛

Wild ginger leaves

¾ ounce (22ml) pear-ginger syrup*
3–4 ounces (90–120ml) dry sparkling wine
Thin slices of pear, for garnish

In a champagne flute or regular wine glass, pour in the pear-ginger syrup. Top with sparkling wine, and garnish with the pear slices.

*Pear-Ginger Syrup
1 cup (235ml) water
1 cup (200g) sugar
1 Forelle pear (or your favorite type), cored and chopped into chunks
½-inch (1-cm) nub of ginger, peeled and chopped

In a saucepan over medium heat, combine the water and sugar. Stir for about a minute or so until the sugar begins to dissolve. Add the pear and ginger, and simmer, stirring occasionally, for about 12 minutes. Allow to cool. Strain the syrup through a fine mesh sieve, transfer to a sealed jar, and store for up to one month in the refrigerator.

SASSAFRAS SIDECAR

When I moved to my house in Staten Island (home of New York's first distillery), the yard came complete with towering sassafras trees, which prolifically produce saplings like they're trying to take over the place. I used to yank them out, cursing their tenacious, soil-gripping nature. Each time I managed to pull one from the soil, I was rewarded with an aroma that made me sigh— something pretty and cheerfully whimsical; a combo of a stick of bubble gum, Fruit Loops, and root beer. A well-meaning friend told me that sassafras contains a poisonous substance, safrole, and to steer clear. Indeed, sassafras was used to make root beer years ago, but the FDA banned it, despite the fact that many have used sassafras for eons as a tonic for myriad maladies. Unless you consume a whole lot of sassafras, though, the likelihood that safrole will be the thing that does you in is a pretty slim margin. Half an ounce (15 milliliters) of syrup in a cocktail is, in my humble opinion, not going to hurt you one little bit. It may even make your weeding a lot more fun when you collect them and simmer up a batch of this syrup. ☞

Sassafras leaves

2 ounces (60ml) cognac or brandy
1 ounce (30ml) cointreau
½ ounce (15ml) sassafras root syrup*
½ ounce (15ml) freshly squeezed lemon juice
1 lemon peel or slice, for garnish

Fill a cocktail shaker half-full with ice cubes. Pour in the brandy or cognac, cointreau, sassafras root syrup, and lemon juice. Shake for 25 to 30 seconds. Strain slowly into an ice-filled rocks glass. Using a standard vegetable peeler, gently slice only the zesty peel of the lemon (avoiding the bitter white pith) above the drink, drop it into the glass, and garnish with an optional lemon slice.

*Sassafras Root Syrup
2 ounces (roughly 60g) sassafras root, washed and chopped
2½ cups (590ml) water
¾ cup (150g) demerara sugar

In a saucepan, simmer the sassafras root in the water for about 25 minutes. Strain the liquid into a heat-proof bowl, discarding the pieces of root, then pour the liquid back into the pan. Add the demerara sugar, and simmer, stirring, until the sugar dissolves. Cool, transfer to a sealed container, and store in the refrigerator for up to six months.

NOTE: If you live in a region where sassafras root doesn't grow in the wild, fear not. Seeds are available for sale in specialty gardening centers, and the root's bark can sometimes be found for sale in packets in dried form. However, if you are unable to get these varieties, try creating your own variation. Vanilla beans with star anise simmered into a simple syrup can make a delicious alternative.

WILDS OF MANHATTAN

—◆◆—

My friends Ray Dowd and Isabel Vincent are always scouring around for wild cocktail garnishes. At his house, Ray has some old crab apple trees, and after a little Googling he presented my husband and me with two jars: one of crab-apple jelly, the other of preserved crab apples for cocktail garnish. I could think of no better occupation for the little, round, cherry-sized red fruits than diving into a Manhattan—really, what better fate is there?

Crab apples ripen in the summer, so you have to plan ahead for this drink. But when you bite into their firm, sweetened flesh after they've lingered in this classic whiskey drink, you'll see it was all worth the (very little) effort.

2 ounces (60ml) rye
1 ounce (30ml) sweet vermouth
2 dashes of Angostura bitters
2 preserved wild crab apples *

Fill a mixing glass half-full with ice cubes. Pour in the rye, vermouth, and bitters and stir for 25 to 30 seconds. Drop in the wild crab apples and strain the cocktail slowly into the glass.

*Preserved Wild Crab Apples
¾ cup (120g) wild crab apples
1½ cups (350ml) water
1½ cups (300g) sugar
½ cup (120ml) brandy

Rinse off the crab apples, then clean the stalks and soak the fruit in water for about half an hour. Drain, and allow to dry. In a pot, simmer the water and sugar until the latter starts to dissolve. Add the crab apples, and simmer for about 15 to 20 minutes. Allow to cool. Stir in the brandy, then ladle the fruit and the liquid into sealable jars. Store in a cool, dry place for up to a year.

MARTIN GOES HIKING

My good friend Mark Zappasodi, a very talented beer maker and grower of hops in Merrimac, Massachusetts, started collecting pine needles from his yard to brew them in beer. "You can do that?!" I asked, surprised, as he handed me a bottle of his latest brewed beauty. Indeed, you can. Because the pine tree is coniferous (meaning that it always has nice, bright green needles), it's at your disposal all year long.

However, not all pine trees are alike: white pines are safe; others are not. Please do not clip off a piece of your Christmas tree and have at it. You must make sure you positively identify your respective source of needles before imbibing anything that might send you to the emergency room with stomach cramps. (Also check on the scarcity of the tree; some trees are struggling with possible extinction—make sure you're judicious in your picking and not contributing to a tree's potential demise.)

This drink is an outdoorsy riff on the Martinez, thought to be the Martini's predecessor. ☞

¼ cup (60ml) white pine-infused Old Tom gin*
¾ ounce (22ml) sweet vermouth
¼ ounce (7ml) maraschino liqueur
1 dash of Angostura bitters
1 sprig of fresh pine needles, for garnish

Fill a mixing glass half-full with ice cubes. Pour in the gin, vermouth (I like my friend Adam Ford's Atsby Armadillo Cake, as it's gloriously spicy and fun), maraschino liqueur, and bitters. Stir for 30 to 45 seconds. Strain slowly into a cocktail or coupe glass and garnish with a sprig of fresh pine needles.

*White Pine–Infused Old Tom Gin
1 cup (roughly 100g) white pine needles
750ml bottle Old Tom gin

In a jar large enough to hold the entire bottle of gin, drop in the pine needles, and muddle them a bit. Pour in the Old Tom gin. Allow to sit in a cool, dark spot for two weeks, then strain out the needles. Keep indefinitely in a cool, dark place.

NOTE: Old Tom gin is the stepping stone between the slightly sweeter genever and drier London dry gin. If you can't find it easily in your local liquor store, cast your shopping net wider. It's worth it!

DIY GIN (MARTINI)

While gin certainly is its own, unique animal in the booze kingdom, it starts out like any neutral spirit: clean, clear, and unadulterated. Basically vodka. What makes gin unique, of course, is all those delicious botanicals infused into it—from the basic to the out-and-out funky. Many new spirit producers are drawn to that unique stamp that can be put on gin; it inspired me, too. So I figured, why not try my hand at a little DIY gin?

The real way to make gin is to allow the rising vapors that evaporate during distillation to seep through a special, perforated basket that holds the roots, herbs, and fruits of choice. But seeing as I don't have a still handy, a workaday ball jar and a little time did just fine. I used botanicals that were dried (juniper berries from my friend Ray Dowd's yard in West Hampton Beach) and fresh (rosemary from my windowsill), and citrus (from, well, the store, since winter is citrus season). I encourage you heartily to come up with your own ideas, too, working in small batches until you create your own signature blend. 🖙

Juniper

2½ ounces (75ml) DIY gin*
½ ounce (15ml) dry vermouth
Orange or lemon peel or sprig of rosemary, for garnish

Fill a mixing glass half-full with ice cubes. Pour in the DIY gin and vermouth and stir for 25 to 30 seconds. Strain slowly into a cocktail glass, and garnish with orange or lemon peel or a sprig of rosemary.

*DIY Gin

2½ tablespoons dried juniper berries
1 tablespoon (15g) coriander
4 cardamom pods, cracked with the thick part of a butcher's knife blade
2 generous peels of lime
2 generous peels of orange or lemon
2 rosemary sprigs
3 cups (710ml) vodka

Drop your botanicals and fruit peels into a quart-sized (1-liter) mason jar. Pour in the vodka, and allow to sit in a cool, dry place for 24 hours. Strain out the botanicals using a fine mesh sieve. Repeat until all traces are removed. Pour the gin back into the mason jar. Keep indefinitely in the sealed jar in a cool, dark place.

VIRGINIA GROWS ROOTS

———✦———

There are few things more warming and smile-inducing than a hot toddy on a freezing-cold day, or when you have a cold. Either way, I'm convinced that if it doesn't cure what ails you, it certainly makes you feel a lot better. These drinks remind me of my mom, Virginia—a nice, Irish-American lass whose very Irish grandmother used to live with her, my uncle, and her parents. When Great-Grandma Casey, as she was known, was sick, this remedy was readily used, and it was one my own mom carried on making for me. Now, don't get me wrong, the amount of whiskey she'd put in one was probably akin to whatever alcohol is in a bottle of store-bought cough medicine. I didn't increase the dosage until I was all grown up. Sassafras, long used for home-remedy medicinal purposes, is known to help you sweat out a cold, but honestly I just like the way it tastes alongside whiskey. ☞

4–6 whole cloves
1 broad strip of lemon peel or wheel
¾ ounce (22ml) sassafrass syrup*
1 ounce (30ml) freshly squeezed lemon juice
1½ ounces (45ml) Irish whiskey
3 ounces (90ml) hot water

Push the sharp point of the whole cloves into the lemon peel or wheel, and drop it into your mug. Add the sassafras syrup, lemon juice, and whiskey. Top with hot water and stir.

*Sassafras Root Syrup
2 ounces (roughly 60g) sassafras root, washed and chopped
2½ cups (590ml) water
¾ cup (150g) demerara sugar

In a saucepan, simmer the sassafras root in the water for about 25 minutes. Strain the liquid into a heat-proof bowl, discarding the pieces of root, then pour the liquid back into the pan. Add the demerara sugar, and simmer, stirring, until the sugar dissolves. Cool, and transfer to a sealed container and store in the refrigerator for up to six months.

NOTE: If you live in a region where sassafras root doesn't grow in the wild, fear not. Seeds are available for sale in specialty gardening centers, and the root's bark can sometimes be found for sale in packets in dried form. However, if you are unable to get these varieties, try creating your own variation. Vanilla beans with star anise simmered into a simple syrup can make a delicious alternative.

HOME FOR THE HOLIDAYS

In my family, the Brandy Alexander reigns supreme as the ultimate holiday cocktail. It's creamy and decadent and smells of spices and a little bit of chocolate. What's not to love? In my husband's family, no Christmas meal is complete without chestnuts roasting on the stovetop. This recipe combines these two festive favorites. The earthy, mildly sweet taste of the nuts infused into brandy is a lovely thing indeed.

Chestnuts generally ripen in the autumn and can be found through December. Grab a bag, head out for a walk through pretty much any park, and be sure to look down; you will be rewarded with a plentiful spread of low-hanging fruit—or, in this case, nuts. ☞

Chestnuts

1½ ounces (45ml) chestnut liqueur*
1 ounce (30ml) crème de cacao
1 ounce (30ml) half and half
1 fresh nutmeg, for garnish

Fill a cocktail shaker half-full with ice cubes. Pour in the chestnut liqueur, crème de cacao, and half and half. Shake for 25 to 30 seconds. Strain slowly into an ice-filled rocks glass. Hold a standard kitchen zester over the glass, and grate a little bit of nutmeg over the top to taste.

*Chestnut Liqueur
1½ pounds (680g) raw chestnuts
2½ cups (590ml) water
1¼ cups (275g) demerara sugar
16 ounces/2 cups (475ml) brandy

Heat the oven to 400°F (200°C). Rinse the chestnuts under cold water, and pat dry. With the flat side of the nut down, carefully use a very sharp kitchen knife to make a slice in the rounded back of the nut. Make one more slice so you score an "X" into the shell. Roast in the oven for about 35 to 40 minutes. (Alternatively, after cutting them, soak them in water, place them on a microwave-safe dish, and nuke 'em for about a minute.) Allow to cool enough so you can pick them up, then peel the shell away.

Pour the water and sugar into a pot set over medium heat. Stir for a minute until the sugar begins to dissolve. Add the chestnuts, and simmer for about 15 minutes. Strain the liquid into a bowl or quart-sized (1-liter) measuring cup. When cool, place the chestnuts in a jar large enough to hold them and your liquid contents. Pour in the reserved cooking syrup and brandy. Allow to sit for ten days to two weeks in a cool, dark place. Strain out the chestnuts using a fine mesh sieve and discard, then pour the liquid into a clean bottle or mason jar. Keep indefinitely.

ACKNOWLEDGMENTS

There's this scene in the movie *Something's Gotta Give* where, portraying a playwright, Diane Keaton locks herself away in her gorgeous Hamptons' beach house, pecking away furiously on her computer in order to finish her manuscript in a fit of gorgeous, beautifully filmed, emotional-rollercoaster turmoil. Occasionally sobbing, sometimes giggling, always impeccably dressed in miraculously unstained white- and cream-colored clothing, and often going for long, thoughtful walks on the beach to contemplate her creative process. The waves crash, the seagulls call, and glasses of crisp Sauvignon Blanc are sipped. She finishes her play and—ta-da!—it's a hit!

Yeah, it's not like that.

The behind-the-scenes of making a book happen is never as romantic or movie-lovely as many people who haven't been through the process think it is. Writing is work; research is work; creating good recipes is work; editing a manuscript is work; photography and illustration are work; negotiating a contract is work. It's far more likely your earnings will buy you a train or bus ticket to the Hamptons—but definitely not a beach house. It's okay if you don't believe me. Everyone who's been through this process—or who has gone through it with me—knows better. For the latter patient, kind, gentle people, I would like to call out some names.

My writer, editor, and booze-biz friends, especially: Lana Bortolot—my ever-faithful friend and travel woobie, Mindy Fox, Elizabeth Goodman, David Lytle, Lew Bryson, Amy Bryant, Shawn Kelley, Lenn Thompson, Carlo DeVito, Adam Ford, Bianca

Miraglia, Allen Katz, for writing such a lovely foreword—good eggs all. You might not even remember some moment when something you said or wrote (or your forgiveness when I totally spaced out) pushed me forward, but it did, and I am grateful.

My editor, Caitlin Doyle—a forager at times herself for this book. I know this was not the easiest project for either of us. Thanks for your cool head and for keeping it on track. Someday, on one continent or another, we will have a very big drink together, my treat.

Josie and Charlie Gueits, my sometime and always wonderful guinea pigs.

Laura Zavatto and Linda Zavatto—you are my heart.

Michael Zavatto, for showing me how to make a proper drink and being a really great dad.

Dan Marotta—for being my best advocate, my best friend, and the best decision I ever made. I love you, always.

HarperCollins Publishers wishes to thank the invaluable team behind the book. Claire Lloyd Davies for her unfading enthusiasm and stamina (in 95°F heat!) and gorgeous photography. Heartfelt gratitude to Jacqui Caulton for her patience and incredible design. Thank you to Amy Zavatto for her beautiful words and recipes. Thank you to Joe Bright, Helena Caldon, and Ben Murphy. Huge thanks to Steve Clarke and Café Van Gogh for lovely foraging adventures around Vauxhall, to OddBins Northcote Road for near-daily boozy assistance, and to the Davies-Stockley household and various Doyle households for beautiful locations (and patience as homes became prop houses!). Finally, a big cheers goes to Essie Cousins, co-conceiver of this project over lunch on a cold day in Hammersmith many moons ago.

INDEX